EASY-TO-COOK

CHICKEN

Carole Handslip

BROCKHAMPTON PRESS
LONDON

First published in Great Britain in 1992 by
Anaya Publishers Ltd,
Strode House, 44–50 Osnaburgh Street, London NW1 3ND

This edition published 1996 by Brockhampton Press,
a member of Hodder Headline PLC Group

Managing Editor: Janet Illsley
Photographer: Clive Streeter
Designer: Pedro Prá-Lopez
Food Stylist: Carole Handslip
Photographic Stylist: Sue Russell

British Library Cataloguing in Publication Data
Rutherford, Lyn
Easy to cook chicken dishes. – (Easy to cook)

ISBN 1 86019 240 8

Typeset in UK by SX Composing Ltd, Rayleigh
Colour reproduction by J. Film Process, Bangkok
Printed in UK by BPC Paulton Books Ltd

NOTES

Ingredients are listed in metric and imperial measures.
Use either set of quantities but not a mixture of both.

All spoon measures are level:
1 tablespoon = one 15 ml spoon
1 teaspoon = one 5 ml spoon.

Use fresh herbs and freshly ground black pepper unless otherwise stated.

Use standard size 3 eggs unless otherwise suggested.

CONTENTS

INTRODUCTION

Time is so valuable and most of us have so many demands on it, that any short cuts – especially in the kitchen – are more than welcome.

Nowadays our supermarkets offer an excellent range of ready prepared cuts of poultry, which are ideal for concocting appetising meals in minutes, rather than hours. Chicken is the perfect choice for the health conscious too, as it is low in fat, high in protein and easily digested. It is also very economical and is probably the most popular of all meats.

The versatile flavour of chicken blends superbly with a number of different herbs, spices, vegetables and fruits. With the wide range of cuts available too, the possibilities are endless.

Chicken breasts can be bought either on the bone or boneless, and with or without skin. They are better consumed without the skin which is the fattening part! Goujons are pieces cut from the underside of the fillet. Quarter chickens, drumsticks, wings or leg joints, thighs, goujons and diced chicken are all available ready-prepared. Chicken livers are usually sold frozen. These are inexpensive and ideal for pâtes and salads; be careful not to overcook them though, or they become tough and hard.

Smoked chicken and smoked turkey are available from most delicatessen counters, and they are sold in slices. Here lies the perfect answer to the quest for the 'five minute meal'.

Poussins – or spring chickens – are tender, very young birds which weigh between 400-500 g (14 oz-1 lb) and each one will feed 1 or 2 people, depending on their appetite.

Like chicken, duck is sold in convenient cuts. You can buy duck breasts, whole breast joints, wings and leg quarters. Turkey is sold as breast steaks or escalopes. It is also available in cubes or strips for stir frys, and as mince which is most useful.

A word about frozen poultry. If you are using frozen poultry make certain that all parts are thoroughly defrosted before cooking. Thaw poultry in its wrappings, piercing a hole through the plastic and placing it on a plate to catch any juices; discard any liquid that gathers. To make quite sure that the meat is thoroughly defrosted, check that the flesh is soft and flexible, and cook as soon as possible after thawing. DO NOT refreeze.

The recipes in this book will show you the wide variety of dishes that you can make from simple cuts of poultry. Whether you need an everyday supper or snack, a sophisticated dinner party dish or something to serve al fresco you should find plenty of ideas here. The one thing that all the recipes have in common is speed, from start to finish. Bon Appetit!

SOUPS & STARTERS

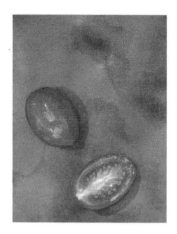

Starters should titillate your taste buds in preparation for the meal to come and, for this reason, they are often piquant. Many of those included here can be served as snacks if you increase the quantities.

Keep a supply of homemade chicken stock on hand in the freezer for making soups. Whenever you have a chicken carcass left over, use it to make stock: put the carcass, or bones, in a saucepan with herbs, a few vegetables and enough water to cover. Simmer gently for 1-1½ hours, then strain and cool. Freeze in convenient quantities.

CONTENTS

SPINACH & CHICKEN SOUP

SERVES 4

You can use cooked chicken for this soup, in which case omit the groundnut oil and add the ginger, garlic and spring onions to the stock with the spinach.

250 g (8 oz) boneless chicken breast, skinned
1 tablespoon groundnut oil
1 cm (½ inch) piece fresh root ginger, chopped
2 cloves garlic, sliced
4 spring onions, diagonally sliced
900 ml (1½ pints) chicken stock
1 tablespoon soy sauce
125 g (4 oz) spinach leaves, shredded
2 tablespoons dry sherry
1 teaspoon sesame oil
salt and pepper to taste

1 Slice the chicken into very thin strips, about 2.5 cm x 5 x 5 mm (1 x ¼ x ¼ inch).

2 Heat the oil in a pan, add the chicken with the ginger, garlic and spring onions and stir fry until the chicken is sealed.

3 Put the stock into a saucepan and bring to the boil. Add the soy sauce and spinach, return to the boil and cook for 2 minutes.

4 Add the chicken mixture, sherry, sesame oil and seasoning. Heat through before serving.

COCK À LEEKIE

SERVES 4

This is a much quicker version of the famous Scottish soup which traditionally uses a capon. Leave out the prunes if you prefer.

25 g (1 oz) butter
500 g (1 lb) leeks, thinly sliced into rings
250 g (8 oz) boneless chicken breast, skinned and
  cut into strips
50 g (2 oz) stoneless prunes, cut into quarters
900 ml (1½ pints) chicken stock
salt and pepper to taste
1 tablespoon chopped parsley

1 Heat the butter in a pan, add the leeks and cook very gently for 10 minutes, stirring occasionally, until softened.

2 Add the chicken, prunes, stock and seasoning. Bring to the boil, cover and simmer for 15 minutes.

3 Stir in the parsley and serve.

CHINESE DUCK SOUP

SERVES 4

The duck should be cut into thin strips so that it cooks quickly. You can use chestnut mushrooms instead of shiitake and spinach instead of pak choi, if you prefer.

50 g (2 oz) thin rice stick noodles, broken into
*   pieces*
2 tablespoons groundnut oil
2 boneless duck breasts, skinned and cut into thin
*   strips*
125 g (4 oz) shiitake mushrooms, thinly sliced
4 spring onions, diagonally sliced
2 cloves garlic, sliced
175 g (6 oz) baby corn cobs, halved lengthways
1.2 litres (2 pints) chicken or duck stock
2 tablespoons soy sauce
salt and pepper to taste
125 g (4 oz) pak choi, shredded
1 teaspoon sesame oil

1 Soak the noodles in boiling water to cover for 10 minutes, then drain.

2 Heat the oil in a pan, add the duck strips and fry briskly for 1-2 minutes. Add the mushrooms, spring onions, garlic and baby corn and stir fry for 1-2 minutes.

3 Add the stock, noodles, soy sauce and seasoning. Bring to the boil and simmer for 1 minute. Add the pak choi and sesame oil and simmer for about 2 minutes. Serve immediately.

CHICKEN NOODLE SOUP

SERVES 4

I frequently make this soup, as I nearly always have chicken stock and leftover chopped chicken in the freezer. Just add vermicelli and herbs and you have a tasty soup.

900 ml (1½ pints) chicken stock
50 g (2 oz) vermicelli, broken up
4 spring onions, sliced
salt and pepper to taste
50 g (2 oz) cooked chicken, chopped
1 tablespoon chopped parsley

1 Put the stock in a saucepan and bring to the boil. Sprinkle in the vermicelli and stir, to ensure it does not stick together, until the stock returns to the boil again.

2 Add the spring onions with seasoning and cook for 6-8 minutes until the pasta is cooked.

3 Add the chopped chicken and parsley and heat through to serve.

SPICED CHICKEN SOUP

SERVES 4

Coconut blends with the spices in this soup to give a creamy subtle piquancy.

1 tablespoon sunflower oil
125 g (4 oz) boneless chicken, skinned and
   shredded
1 onion, thinly sliced
50 g (2 oz) okra, sliced
1 clove garlic, chopped
½ teaspoon turmeric
½ teaspoon chilli powder
600 ml (1 pint) chicken stock
50 g (2 oz) creamed coconut, blended with
   150 ml (¼ pint) boiling water
50 g (2 oz) long grain rice
salt and pepper to taste
2 tablespoons chopped coriander leaves

1 Heat the oil in a saucepan and stir fry the chicken until sealed, then remove from the pan with a slotted spoon.

2 Add the onion and okra to the pan and fry for about 5 minutes until softened.

3 Stir in the garlic, turmeric and chilli powder and cook for 30 seconds.

4 Add the stock, blended coconut and rice and bring to the boil. Cover and simmer gently for 15 minutes.

5 Add the chicken with seasoning and cook for a further 5 minutes. Stir in the chopped coriander and serve.

TURKEY CONSOMMÉ JULIENNE

SERVES 4

Canned consommé makes an excellent base for this instant soup. It looks most attractive if you cut the vegetables and turkey into julienne strips, or matchstick sized pieces, but the flavour will be just as good if you chop them roughly.

1 carrot
1 stick celery
2 spring onions
295 g (10.4 oz) can condensed consommé
50 g (2 oz) cooked turkey, cut into thin strips
2 tablespoons dry sherry
1 tablespoon chopped parsley
salt and pepper to taste

1 Cut the carrot, celery and spring onions into matchstick pieces, 2.5 cm x 3mm x 3mm (1 x 1/8 x 1/8 inch).

2 Put the vegetables in a large pan with 450 ml (¾ pint) water and a little salt. Bring to the boil and simmer for 5 minutes.

3 Add the consommé, turkey and sherry with the parsley and seasoning to taste and simmer for 2 minutes to heat through.

ICED CHICKEN & ALMOND SOUP

SERVES 4

A subtle blend of almond and chicken with juicy muscat grapes, this soup is extremely quick to make in a blender. Leave it to chill for as long as possible, or alternatively serve immediately – with a few ice cubes floating in each portion.

125 g (4 oz) cooked chicken, chopped
1 small clove garlic, crushed
125 g (4 oz) ground almonds
600 ml (1 pint) milk
salt and pepper to taste
1 teaspoon lemon juice (approximately)
125 g (4 oz) muscat grapes, halved and seeded
1 teaspoon chopped dill

1 Put the chicken, garlic, ground almonds, milk and seasoning in a blender and blend until mixture is smooth.

2 Turn into a bowl and add lemon juice to taste. Cover and chill for 30 minutes.

3 Spoon into individual soup bowls and sprinkle with the grapes and dill to serve.

Note Although you can purée this soup in a food processor, it does not give such a fine smooth texture as a blender.

CHICKEN & AVOCADO MOUSSE

SERVES 4-6

This mousse is very quick to make using a food processor, but you need to leave it to set for an hour before turning out; 15 minutes will be sufficient if you serve it in the ramekins.

125 g (4 fl oz) hot chicken stock
2 teaspoons gelatine, soaked in 2 tablespoons
  cold water
1 large avocado, halved, stoned and peeled
75 g (3 oz) fromage frais
1 teaspoon finely chopped spring onion
1 teaspoon lemon juice
1 teaspoon Worcestershire sauce
salt and pepper to taste
125 g (4 oz) smoked chicken, finely chopped
4 tablespoons single cream

TO GARNISH
few avocado slices
fennel sprigs

1 Add the hot stock to the soaked gelatine and stir until dissolved.

2 Roughly chop the avocado and put into a food processor with the fromage frais, spring onion, lemon juice, Worcestershire sauce and seasoning. Blend until smooth.

3 Pour into a bowl and stir in the chicken, dissolved gelatine and cream.

4 Divide between 4-6 small greased ramekins and chill for 1 hour or until set.

5 Turn out on to individual plates and garnish with avocado slices and fennel to serve.

CHICKEN & AVOCADO WITH BACON DRESSING

SERVES 4

A delicious blend of textures and flavours. Arrange the salad before you make the dressing, so you can apply the dressing and serve immediately, while still warm.

1 large avocado, halved, stoned and peeled
150 g (5 oz) cooked chicken breast, sliced

WARM BACON DRESSING
2 tablespoons olive oil
75 g (3 oz) smoked streaky bacon, derinded and chopped
1 tablespoon tarragon vinegar
1 tablespoon capers

TO GARNISH
tarragon sprigs

1 Slice the avocado thinly and arrange the slices alternately with the chicken, overlapping on individual plates.

2 To make the dressing, heat the oil in a frying pan and fry the bacon until golden and crisp.

3 Remove from the heat, add the vinegar and capers and immediately pour over the salad. Garnish with tarragon sprigs. Serve whilst still warm, with brown bread and butter.

CHICKEN LIVER & PEPPERCORN PÂTÉ

SERVES 6

If you want to keep this pâté for a few days, pack it into a small china serving dish, smooth the surface and pour clarified butter over the top to cover completely.

2 tablespoons olive oil
1 onion, chopped
250 g (8 oz) chicken livers, trimmed
2 cloves garlic, chopped
125 g (4 oz) melted butter
1 tablespoon brandy
1 tablespoon chopped parsley
1 teaspoon chopped thyme
salt and pepper to taste
1 tablespoon green peppercorns in brine, drained

TO SERVE
thyme sprigs and green peppercorns to garnish
toast fingers or melba toast

1 Heat the oil in a pan, add the onion and fry gently until softened.

2 Add the chicken livers and garlic and cook for 8-10 minutes.

3 Transfer the mixture to a blender or food processor. Add the melted butter, brandy, herbs and seasoning, and blend until smooth. Add the peppercorns and blend for a few seconds until mixture is evenly combined.

4 Spoon the pâté on to individual serving dishes and garnish with thyme and peppercorns. Serve with toast.

ABOVE: CHICKEN & AVOCADO WITH BACON DRESSING *BELOW*: CHICKEN LIVER & PEPPERCORN PÂTÉ

CHICKEN & MUSHROOM PUFFS

SERVES 4

1 tablespoon olive oil
15 g (½ oz) butter
175 g (6 oz) boneless chicken, skinned and cubed
175 g (6 oz) mushrooms, quartered
2 cloves garlic, chopped
1 tablespoon flour
125 ml (4 fl oz) chicken stock
2 tablespoons double cream
2 tablespoons chopped chives
salt and pepper to taste
250 g (8 oz) packet puff pastry
beaten egg to glaze

1 Preheat oven to 220°C (425°F/Gas 7).

2 Heat the oil and butter in a pan, add the chicken, mushrooms and garlic and fry briskly for 3-4 minutes, stirring constantly.

3 Stir in flour, then add stock and bring to the boil. Cook, stirring, for 2 minutes until thickened.

4 Stir in the cream, chives and seasoning and divide between 4 ramekins. Let cool.

5 Roll out the pastry and cut out four 8.5 cm (3½ inch) circles (i.e. slightly larger than the ramekins), using a plain cutter.

6 Dampen the edges of the ramekins and position the pastry lids on top. Press the edges to seal. Make a hole in the centre of each pie and brush with beaten egg. Decorate with leaves cut from the pastry trimmings if liked. Brush with egg. Bake in the oven for 15 minutes until golden and well risen. Serve immediately.

CHICKEN GOUJONS WITH TARTARE SAUCE

SERVES 6

These crisp little fingers of chicken accompanied by a piquant sauce make a delicious starter.

250 g (8 oz) chicken goujons
1 egg, beaten
50 g (2 oz) fresh breadcrumbs
oil for deep frying

TARTARE SAUCE
3 tablespoons fromage frais
3 tablespoons mayonnaise
1 tablespoon chopped capers
1 tablespoon chopped gherkins
1 tablespoon chopped chives
1 tablespoon chopped parsley
salt and pepper to taste

TO GARNISH
fennel sprigs

1 To make the tartare sauce, mix all the ingredients together in a bowl until smooth.

2 Cut each goujon into long pieces. Dip each piece into the egg, then toss in the breadcrumbs to coat completely.

3 Heat the oil in a deep fryer to 180°C (350°F), or until a cube of bread dropped in turns brown in 30 seconds.

4 Put the goujons in the frying basket, lower into the hot oil and fry for 2 minutes until crisp and golden. Drain thoroughly on kitchen paper. Serve immediately garnished with fennel and accompanied by the tartare sauce.

ABOVE: CHICKEN GOUJONS WITH TARTARE SAUCE *BELOW:* CHICKEN & MUSHROOM PUFFS

CHICKEN & PROSCIUTTO BASKETS

SERVES 4

These filo pastry baskets look complicated, but are very quick and easy to prepare. They make a most impressive starter, and you can use them to enclose a variety of fillings.

4 -5 sheets filo pastry
6 tablespoons fromage frais
1 tablespoon chopped tarragon
1/2 teaspoon clear honey
1 teaspoon tarragon vinegar
salt and pepper to taste
125 g (4 oz) cooked chicken, cubed
25 g (1 oz) prosciutto, cut into squares
50 g (2 oz) green grapes, halved and seeded

TO GARNISH
tarragon sprigs

1. Preheat oven to 190°C (375°F/Gas 5).

2. Cut the filo pastry into twelve 10 cm (4 inch) squares. Stack in a pile and cover with a tea towel to prevent them drying out.

3. Invert 4 dariole moulds on a baking sheet. Drape 3 squares of pastry over each one, turning each square at a slight angle to the last.

4. Bake for 6-8 minutes until golden brown. Leave to cool, then carefully ease each filo basket off the tin with a small knife.

5. To make the filling, mix the fromage frais with the tarragon, honey, vinegar and seasoning. Stir in the chicken, prosciutto and grapes.

6. Spoon the filling into the filo baskets and garnish with tarragon to serve.

DUCK BREASTS WITH REDCURRANT VINAIGRETTE

SERVES 4

4 duck breasts
oil for brushing

REDCURRANT VINAIGRETTE
125 g (4 oz) redcurrants
1 teaspoon redcurrant jelly
2 tablespoons olive oil
1 tablespoon lemon juice
salt and pepper to taste

TO SERVE
1 head chicory
handful of rocket leaves
redcurrant sprigs to garnish

1. Preheat the grill to medium. Place the duck breasts, skin side down, on a rack in a grill pan. Brush with oil and grill for 3-4 minutes. Turn the duck over and cook for a further 5-7 minutes until the skin crispens and most of the fat has run out, but the inside flesh is still slightly pink.

2. Meanwhile make the vinaigrette. Press the redcurrants and jelly through a nylon sieve into a bowl. Mix in the oil, lemon juice and seasoning.

3. Arrange the chicory and rocket leaves on 4 serving plates. Slice the warm duck breasts thinly and arrange in overlapping slices next to the salad.

4. Pour the vinaigrette over the salad and duck. Garnish with redcurrants and serve with brown bread and butter.

ABOVE: DUCK BREASTS WITH REDCURRANT VINAIGRETTE *BELOW*: CHICKEN & PROSCIUTTO BASKETS

TURKEY & BACON KEBABS

SERVES 4

I prefer to use smoked bacon to wrap round the turkey. I also like to cook these kebabs until the bacon is really crisp.

6 rashers smoked streaky bacon, derinded
75 g (3 oz) boneless turkey, cubed

SAUCE
75 g (3 oz) fromage frais
2 teaspoons horseradish sauce
2 teaspoons coarse grain (Meaux) mustard
salt and pepper to taste

TO GARNISH
salad leaves

1. Stretch the bacon with the back of a knife, then cut each rasher into 3 pieces.

2. Wrap each piece of bacon round a cube of turkey and thread on to 4 skewers.

3. To make the sauce, mix the fromage frais with the horseradish, mustard and seasoning.

4. Preheat the grill to medium. Put the kebabs on a rack in a grill pan and grill for 8-10 minutes, turning once, until the bacon is crisp.

5. Serve immediately, garnished with salad leaves, and accompanied by the sauce.

HONEY GLAZED CHICKEN WINGS

SERVES 4

A starter with a Chinese flavour, which can be cooked on a barbecue. As these tasty chicken wings are best eaten with your fingers, make sure you have plenty of napkins to hand.

8 chicken wings

GLAZE
2 tablespoons clear honey
1 tablespoon tomato sauce
2 tablespoons hoisin sauce

PEKING CUCUMBER
1/2 cucumber, peeled and sliced
2 tablespoons rice wine or cider vinegar
1 teaspoon soy sauce
1/2 teaspoon salt

TO GARNISH
shredded spring onion

1. For the glaze, mix together the honey, tomato and hoisin sauces in a bowl. Brush over the chicken wings to coat completely.

2. To prepare the Peking Cucumber, cut the cucumber slices into quarters and place in a bowl with the vinegar, soy sauce and salt. Stir well, then leave to stand for 15 minutes, stirring occasionally.

3. Preheat the grill to medium. Put the chicken wings on a rack in the grill pan and grill for 8-10 minutes until well cooked and dark brown, turning once. Serve immediately, garnished with spring onion and accompanied by the Peking Cucumber.

ABOVE: HONEY GLAZED CHICKEN WINGS *BELOW*: TURKEY & BACON KEBABS

SALADS

Chicken, duck and turkey can all be used to excellent effect in salads and, as you only need a small quantity, this is an ideal way to use up leftovers. Try Italian pasta salad, flavoured with basil, olives and lashings of garlic dressing; or Oriental chicken salad, with mangetout, mushrooms and baby corn, tossed in a sesame dressing.

To save time, keep a bottle of ready prepared French dressing in the storecupboard – just add flavourings as you need them – a generous helping of Meaux mustard, a tablespoon or two of chopped herbs, or a crushed garlic clove – to complement the chosen salad.

CONTENTS

ORIENTAL CHICKEN SALAD

SERVES 4

This is a substantial salad – suitable for a light lunch.

250 g (8 oz) mangetout, topped and tailed
250 g (8 oz) baby corn, halved lengthways
350 g (12 oz) cooked chicken, cut into strips
4 spring onions, cut into julienne strips
1 red pepper, cored, seeded and cut into strips
125 g (4 oz) mushrooms, sliced
25 g (1 oz) cashew nuts, toasted

SESAME DRESSING
2 tablespoons tahini (sesame seed paste)
2 tablespoons rice or wine vinegar
2 tablespoons medium sherry
1 tablespoon soy sauce
1 teaspoon sesame oil
1 clove garlic, crushed
salt and pepper to taste

1 Blanch the mangetout and baby corn in boiling water for 3 minutes. Drain and rinse under cold water, then drain thoroughly.

2 Place in a bowl with the chicken, spring onions, red pepper and mushrooms. Toss to mix.

3 To make the dressing, put the sesame paste in a bowl and gradually mix in the vinegar and sherry. Add the soy sauce, sesame oil and garlic and mix together thoroughly, adding seasoning to taste.

4 Pour the dressing over the salad, toss well and sprinkle with the nuts to serve.

DUCK & ORANGE SALAD

SERVES 4

Boneless duck breasts are best grilled until the skin is crisp and most of the fat has run out. I like to serve the flesh slightly pink, but you can cook it for a few minutes longer than suggested if you prefer.

4 duck breasts, about 150 g (5 oz) each
oil for brushing
2 tablespoons pine nuts, toasted

ORANGE DRESSING
3 tablespoons olive oil
2 tablespoons concentrated orange juice
1 tablespoon chopped chives
salt and pepper to taste

SALAD
3 heads chicory, sliced diagonally
2 oranges, peeled and cut into segments
1 bunch watercress

1 Preheat the grill to medium. Place the duck breasts, skin side down, on a rack in the grill pan. Brush with oil and grill for 3-4 minutes. Turn the duck over and cook for 5-6 minutes until the skin has crispened.

2 Meanwhile, shake the dressing ingredients in a screw-topped jar to mix.

3 Put the salad ingredients in a bowl, pour over half of the dressing and toss well.

4 Slice the duck thinly and arrange overlapping slices on one side of each serving plate. Spoon over the remaining dressing.

5 Arrange the salad next to the duck and sprinkle with toasted pine nuts to serve.

ARTICHOKE & CHICKEN SALAD

SERVES 4

Use quality black olives in this salad as their flavour is quite dominant. Canned artichokes in brine can be used in place of artichokes in oil, but the latter have a better flavour. Serve this tasty salad with plenty of crusty bread.

350 g (12 oz) cooked chicken
6 tomatoes, skinned and cut into wedges
50 g (2 oz) black olives, halved and stoned
275 g (9 oz) bottled artichokes in oil, drained
  and quartered
2 tablespoons chopped basil

CAPER DRESSING
4 tablespoons olive oil
2 tablespoons wine vinegar
2 cloves garlic, crushed
1 tablespoon coarse grain (Meaux) mustard
½ teaspoon clear honey
1 tablespoon chopped capers
salt and pepper to taste

TO GARNISH
curly endive (frisée)

1 To make the dressing, put all the ingredients in a screw-topped jar and shake together thoroughly until blended.

2 Cut the chicken into pieces, put into a bowl, pour over the dressing and leave to marinate for 10 minutes.

3 Add the tomatoes, olives, artichokes and basil. Toss well to mix and turn into a serving dish. Garnish with curly endive.

TURKEY TONNATO

SERVES 4

Slices of turkey coated in a tuna fish sauce – an adaptation of an Italian recipe that features veal.

500 g (1 lb) cooked turkey
4 curled radicchio leaves

TUNA FISH SAUCE
75 g (3 oz) can tuna fish, drained
125 g (4 oz) fromage frais
1 tablespoon anchovy essence
1 tablespoon lemon juice
salt and pepper to taste
4 tablespoons mayonnaise
a little milk (optional)

TO GARNISH
1 tablespoon capers
lemon slices
herb sprigs

1 To make the sauce, put the tuna fish and fromage frais in a food processor or blender with the anchovy essence, lemon juice and seasoning. Blend until the mixture is smooth. Fold into the mayonnaise, adding a little milk if the mixture becomes too stiff.

2 Cut the turkey into finger sized pieces and mix with half of the tuna sauce.

3 Place a curled radicchio leaf on each serving plate. Spoon some turkey mixture into each leaf and spoon the remaining tuna sauce over the top. Garnish with capers, lemon slices and herbs to serve.

ABOVE: ARTICHOKE & CHICKEN SALAD *BELOW*: TURKEY TONNATO

SALADE TIÈDE

SERVES 4

This is one of my favourite summer salads, and it is so quick to prepare. Have all the salad leaves ready and simply fry the bacon and chicken livers just before you're ready to eat.

1 oak leaf lettuce
½ curly endive (frisée)
few radicchio leaves
few rocket leaves
2 heads chicory, diagonally sliced
3 tablespoons olive oil
2 cloves garlic, sliced
125 g (4 oz) smoked streaky bacon, derinded and cut into strips
250 g (8 oz) chicken livers
3 tablespoons cider vinegar
salt and pepper to taste
50 g (2 oz) chopped walnuts

1 Tear the lettuce, endive and radicchio into manageable sized pieces and put into a salad bowl with the rocket leaves and chicory.

2 Heat the oil in a frying pan, add the garlic, bacon and chicken livers and fry for 5-6 minutes until tender but still pink inside, stirring occasionally.

3 Slice the chicken livers and scatter over the salad with the bacon.

4 Pour the vinegar into the pan and stir round to mix with the liver juices. Add seasoning, then pour over the salad. Sprinkle the chopped walnuts on top to serve.

CHICKEN & BROCCOLI SALAD

SERVES 4

You can use any blue cheese for this dressing. Stilton makes an excellent alternative.

125 g (4 oz) cauliflower
250 g (8 oz) broccoli
350 g (12 oz) cooked chicken, cut into strips
125 g (4 oz) streaky bacon, derinded and chopped

ROQUEFORT DRESSING
50 g (2 oz) Roquefort
150 ml (¼ pint) single cream
2 tablespoons chopped chives
salt and pepper to taste

1 Break the cauliflower and broccoli into small florets and cook in boiling salted water for 4 minutes. Drain thoroughly and put into a bowl with the chicken.

2 Fry the bacon in its own fat until crisp; drain and set aside.

3 To make the dressing, mash the cheese with a fork and gradually mix in the cream to form a smooth paste. Stir in the chives and seasoning.

4 Pour the dressing over the salad and toss well to coat completely. Turn into a shallow serving dish and sprinkle with the bacon to serve.

SPICED CHICKEN & PASTA MAYONNAISE

SERVES 4

Choose a mild or hot curry sauce depending on your taste. The spices in bottled curry sauces have been pre-fried in oil, so need no further cooking.

---

75 g (3 oz) pasta shells
350 g (12 oz) cooked chicken
125 g (4 oz) can pineapple chunks, drained
50g (2 oz) split blanched almonds, toasted and chopped
1 tablespoon chopped coriander leaves

CURRY MAYONNAISE
1 tablespoon concentrated curry sauce
1 tablespoon clear honey
2 teaspoons tomato purée
150 ml (¼ pint) mayonnaise
125 g (4 oz) fromage frais
salt and pepper to taste

TO GARNISH
coriander sprigs
pineapple slices

1 Cook the pasta in plenty of boiling salted water for 10-12 minutes until al dente. Drain, rinse under cold water, then drain thoroughly. Turn pasta into a bowl.

2 Cut the chicken into chunks, then add to the pasta with the pineapple.

3 To prepare the curry mayonnaise, mix the curry sauce, honey and tomato purée together in a bowl. Add the mayonnaise and fromage frais and stir until evenly blended. Check the seasoning.

4 Add the curry mayonnaise to the salad and mix well. Serve sprinkled with the nuts and chopped coriander. Garnish with coriander and pineapple.

CHICKEN, CELERY & HAM SALAD

SERVES 4

Chicken and smoked ham combined with crunchy apples and celery in a tasty yogurt dressing, that retains the flavour of mayonnaise but has half of the fat content.

---

2 Cox's apples
250 g (8 oz) cooked chicken, chopped
2 sticks celery, thinly sliced
125 g (4 oz) smoked ham, chopped
25 g (1 oz) hazelnuts, roughly chopped and toasted
½ head curly endive (frisée)

YOGURT MAYONNAISE
6 tablespoons mayonnaise
6 tablespoons Greek yogurt
2 tablespoons chopped chives

TO GARNISH
few apple slices
chives

1 To make the yogurt mayonnaise, mix all the ingredients together in a bowl until smooth.

2 Quarter the apples, discard the cores, then chop roughly. Place in a bowl with the chicken, celery and ham. Pour in the yogurt mayonnaise and toss until the salad is well coated.

3 Turn on to a serving dish, sprinkle with the nuts and surround with the curly endive. Garnish with apple slices and chives. Serve with crusty bread.

ABOVE: CHICKEN, CELERY & HAM SALAD *BELOW*: SPICED CHICKEN & PASTA MAYONNAISE

ITALIAN PASTA SALAD

SERVES 4

Make sure you drain the pasta really thoroughly to avoid diluting the dressing.

75 g (3 oz) pasta spirals
350 g (12 oz) cooked chicken
6 tomatoes, skinned and cut into wedges
2 sun dried tomatoes, drained and cut into strips
    (optional)
50 g (2 oz) black olives, halved and stoned
125 g (4 oz) Mozzarella cheese, drained and
    cubed
4 spring onions, thinly sliced
2 tablespoons chopped parsley
2 tablespoons chopped basil
basil leaves to garnish

GARLIC DRESSING
2 tablespoons olive oil
2 tablespoons double cream
1 tablespoon wine vinegar
2 cloves garlic, crushed
2 teaspoons French mustard
1 teaspoon clear honey
salt and pepper to taste

1 Cook the pasta in plenty of boiling salted water for 10-12 minutes until al dente. Drain and rinse under cold water, then drain thoroughly.

2 To make the garlic dressing, put all the ingredients in a screw-topped jar and shake vigorously to mix.

3 Cut the chicken into pieces, add to the pasta then pour over the dressing and mix thoroughly. Add all the remaining salad ingredients and toss well. Serve garnished with basil leaves.

SPICED RICE & CHICKEN SALAD

SERVES 4-6

A useful salad using leftover chicken and rice. If you forget to soak the apricots you can use sultanas or dates instead. To obtain this quantity of cooked rice you will need to boil 175 g (6 oz) raw weight.

1 tablespoon sunflower oil
50 g (2 oz) split blanched almonds
seeds of 6 cardamom pods
1/2 teaspoon ground cinnamon
1 teaspoon ground cumin
500 g (1 lb 2 oz) cooked Basmati rice
175 g (6 oz) cooked chicken, cubed
4 sticks celery, chopped
4 spring onions, chopped
75 g (3 oz) dried apricots, soaked overnight
4 tablespoons garlic dressing (see opposite)
1 tablespoon chopped parsley or coriander

TO GARNISH
coriander leaves

1 Heat the oil in a small pan, add the almonds and fry until they begin to turn golden. Add the spices and fry for a further few seconds.

2 Put the rice in a bowl, add the almonds and spices, then stir in the chicken, celery and spring onions.

3 Drain the apricots and chop, then add to the salad with the dressing. Toss well to coat and sprinkle with chopped parsley or coriander. Garnish with coriander leaves.

SNACKS & LIGHT MEALS

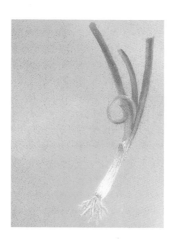

Here you will find suggestions for all kinds of quick and easy snacks, including ideas for using up leftover chicken. Instant snacks – on toast, bagels and rolls – are also included. Try pan bagna or sesame turkey toasts, for something a bit different.

Hearty soups make satisfying snack meals – chicken and sweetcorn chowder, for example. You can also use canned beans, vegetables and leftover chicken to make simple soups more sustaining. Serve interesting flavoured breads and rolls to accompany your snacks.

CONTENTS

CROUSTADES

SERVES 4

1 large (unsliced) wholemeal sandwich loaf
3 tablespoons sunflower oil

FILLING
250 g (8 oz) asparagus spears
2 tablespoons sunflower oil
1 onion, chopped
75 g (3 oz) mushrooms, sliced
2 tablespoons flour
225 ml (8 fl oz) chicken stock
250 g (8 oz) cooked chicken, cubed
2 tablespoons single cream
1 tablespoon chopped tarragon
salt and pepper to taste

1 Preheat oven to 200°C (400°F/Gas 6).

2 Cut four 3.5 cm (1½ inch) thick slices from the loaf, then cut a 10 cm (4 inch) square from the middle of each one. Using a sharp knife, hollow out the centres, leaving a 1 cm (½ inch) border and base.

3 Brush the croustades all over with the oil, place on a baking sheet and bake in the oven for 10 minutes until crisp.

4 Cut the asparagus into 4 cm (1½ inch) lengths, keeping the tips separate. Cook the stalks in boiling salted water for 4 minutes, then add the tips and cook for a further 3 minutes.

5 Heat the oil in a pan, add the onion and mushrooms and cook for 3 minutes. Stir in the flour, then gradually stir in the stock. Bring to the boil and cook, stirring, for 2 minutes.

6 Add the chicken, cream, tarragon and seasoning. Spoon into the croustades and serve immediately, with a green salad.

CHICKEN & TOMATO SCRAMBLE

SERVES 4

This pan-fried scrambled egg is an adaptation of a Turkish breakfast dish. Use parsley instead of basil if you prefer.

1 tablespoon olive oil
15 g (½ oz) butter
4 spring onions, thinly sliced
350 g (12 oz) tomatoes, skinned and chopped
salt and pepper to taste
6 eggs
250 g (8 oz) cooked chicken, chopped
2 tablespoons chopped basil

TO SERVE
toast triangles

1 Heat the oil and butter in a frying pan, add the spring onions and fry, stirring, for 1 minute. Add the tomatoes and seasoning and cook for 2 minutes.

2 Beat the eggs in a bowl, add the chicken and basil, then pour the mixture into the pan.

3 Stir lightly to mix and cook gently, stirring occasionally as the egg sets.

4 Turn on to individual plates and serve immediately, with triangles of toast.

ABOVE: CHICKEN & TOMATO SCRAMBLE *BELOW*: CROUSTADES

OMELETTE CRÊPES WITH TURKEY & HAM

SERVES 4

These little omelettes – filled with a creamy turkey mixture – are perfect for a light lunch served with a salad. You can, of course, use cooked chicken instead of turkey.

OMELETTE CRÊPES
2 tablespoons water
2 teaspoons cornflour
4 eggs
salt and pepper to taste

FILLING
2 tablespoons oil
125 g (4 oz) mushrooms, sliced
4 spring onions, thinly sliced
1 clove garlic, chopped
1½ tablespoons flour
175 ml (6 fl oz) milk
125 g (4 oz) cooked turkey, chopped
50 g (2 oz) ham, chopped
1 tablespoon chopped parsley
salt and pepper to taste

TO GARNISH
parsley sprigs

1 First prepare the filling. Heat the oil in a pan, add the mushrooms, spring onions and garlic and stir fry for 2 minutes.

2 Remove from the heat, stir in the flour, then add the milk, stirring until blended. Bring to the boil and cook, stirring, for 2 minutes until thickened.

3 Stir in the turkey, ham, parsley and seasoning; keep warm.

4 For the omelette crêpe mixture, blend the water with the cornflour until smooth. Beat in the eggs and seasoning.

5 Heat a 20 cm (8 inch) omelette pan and brush with a little oil. Pour in a quarter of the egg mixture, tilting the pan to spread it evenly. Cook over moderate heat until the underside is golden brown and the top is set.

6 Loosen and slide on to a warm plate. Cover with a quarter of the filling, fold over and keep warm.

7 Repeat with the remaining mixture to make three more omelette crêpes.

8 Garnish with parsley and serve with French bread and butter and a crisp green salad.

VARIATION Omit the mushrooms from the filling. Add 2 skinned, seeded and chopped tomatoes with the turkey and ham.

CHICKEN LIVER BAGELS

SERVES 2 OR 4

Serve one or two bagel halves per person depending on appetite. You could put a dill pickle half in the centre of each bagel half instead of a cherry tomato if you prefer.

2 tablespoons olive oil
1 onion, chopped
2 cloves garlic, chopped
250 g (8 oz) chicken livers
1 tablespoon chopped parsley
1 teaspoon chopped thyme
salt and pepper to taste
2 bagels
25 g (1 oz) butter
4 cherry tomatoes

TO GARNISH
herb sprigs

1. Heat the oil in a pan, add the onion and cook gently until softened.

2. Add the garlic and chicken livers and sauté for 6-8 minutes until the livers are almost cooked through but still slightly pink inside, adding the herbs and seasoning for the last 2 minutes.

3. Chop the livers roughly then return to the pan to keep warm.

4. Halve the bagels and toast the cut sides. Spread with butter and put a cherry tomato in the centre of each half.

5. Spoon the liver mixture on top and garnish with herbs. Serve with a crisp salad.

PAN BAGNA

SERVES 4

A popular snack served in cafés all over Provence. Crisp rolls or baguettes are soaked in garlicy olive oil and – in this version – filled with chicken and salad.

4 long crisp rolls
120 ml (4 fl oz) olive oil
2 cloves garlic, crushed
salt and pepper to taste
1 beefsteak tomato, sliced
¼ cucumber, sliced
½ small onion, thinly sliced
125 g (4 oz) cooked chicken breast, sliced
16 black olives, halved and stoned
few lettuce leaves

1. Split the rolls along one side without cutting right through the crust, then open them out so that they lie flat.

2. Mix together the oil, garlic and seasoning, then drizzle over the cut surfaces of the bread and press in evenly.

3. Sandwich together with the tomato, cucumber, onion, chicken, olives and lettuce. Close the two halves pressing firmly together, and wrap the rolls in foil until required.

ABOVE: PAN BAGNA *BELOW:* CHICKEN LIVER BAGELS

CHICKEN PÂTÉ

SERVES 4

An ideal quick way to use up all those leftover chicken pieces. You can use smoked ham instead of prosciutto and rye bread instead of pumpernickel if you prefer.

250 g (8 oz) cooked chicken, in pieces
125 g (4 oz) fromage frais
1 tablespoon chopped tarragon
1 tablespoon chopped parsley
salt and pepper to taste
25 g (1 oz) prosciutto, chopped

TO SERVE
8 slices pumpernickel
4 dill pickles, sliced lengthways
2 tomatoes, sliced
parsley sprigs

1 Put the chicken, fromage frais, herbs and seasoning in a food processor and blend until the mixture is smooth.

2 Turn the mixture into a bowl and stir in the chopped prosciutto.

3 Spread the pumpernickel with the pâté. Cut each slice in half and arrange the dill pickle and tomato slices on top. Garnish with parsley.

SMOKED CHICKEN & CHEESE TOASTS

SERVES 4

I particularly like the combination of smoked chicken and goat's cheese, but you could use ordinary cooked chicken with Gruyère or Cheddar cheese. A very quick and delicious snack.

8 slices coarse grain rye bread
125 g (4 oz) smoked chicken or turkey, sliced
175 g (6 oz) goat's cheese, thinly sliced
herb sprigs to garnish

1 Preheat the grill and toast the bread on one side only.

2 Arrange the chicken or turkey on the untoasted side. Place slices of goat's cheese on top.

3 Grill under a moderate heat until the cheese is beginning to turn brown. Serve immediately, garnished with herbs.

CHICKEN SATAY

SERVES 4

*500 g (1 lb) boneless chicken, skinned and cut
  into 1 cm (½ inch) cubes*

MARINADE
3 tablespoons soy sauce
1 tablespoon lemon juice
1 clove garlic, crushed
2 teaspoons clear honey
2 teaspoons sesame oil

PEANUT SAUCE
2 tablespoons groundnut oil
1 onion, chopped
2 cloves garlic, chopped
1 teaspoon ground cumin
1 teaspoon ground coriander
½ teaspoon chilli powder
225 ml (8 fl oz) tomato juice
1 tablespoon soy sauce
3-4 tablespoons crunchy peanut butter

1 Mix together the marinade ingredients. Put the chicken cubes in a bowl, pour over the marinade and leave for 1 hour.

2 To make the sauce, heat the oil in a pan and fry the onion until softened. Add the garlic and spices and cook for 1 minute, then pour in the tomato juice and soy sauce.

3 Stir in the peanut butter until evenly blended and cook for 3 minutes to thicken.

4 Preheat the grill to medium. Remove the chicken cubes from the marinade and thread on to 8 bamboo skewers. Grill for 3-4 minutes on each side until cooked through. Serve with the peanut sauce.

SESAME TURKEY TOASTS

SERVES 4

Minced turkey is available from supermarkets. Used in this way, it makes an interesting snack.

125 g (4 oz) minced turkey
½ egg white
2 spring onions, finely chopped
1 teaspoon sesame oil
½ teaspoon five-spice powder
salt and pepper to taste
4 slices bread
25 g (1 oz) sesame seeds
oil for deep frying

1 Mix the turkey, egg white, spring onions, sesame oil, five-spice powder and seasoning together to form a smooth paste.

2 Spread a 1 cm (½ inch) thick layer of turkey mixture on each slice of bread. Cut each slice into 3 fingers.

3 Dip each piece into the sesame seeds to coat the filling completely.

4 Heat the oil in a deep fryer to 180°C (350°F), or until a cube of bread dropped in browns in 30 seconds.

5 Fry the sesame fingers, a few at a time, for 3-4 minutes until golden brown on both sides. Drain thoroughly on kitchen paper. Serve hot.

CHICKEN FRITTATA

SERVES 4

A frittata is an Italian omelette which has all sorts of different ingredients incorporated within the egg mixture. It may be thin or thick like this one, and may be fried on both sides or finished under the grill, as I have suggested here.

2 tablespoons olive oil
125 g (4 oz) streaky bacon, chopped
1 onion, chopped
6 eggs
salt and pepper to taste
250 g (8 oz) cooked chicken, chopped
2 tablespoons chopped parsley

1 Heat half the oil in a 23 cm (9 inch) omelette pan, add the bacon and onion and fry until they are golden.

2 Break the eggs into a bowl and season. Add the chicken, parsley and fried onion mixture and mix together.

3 Add the remaining oil to the pan and heat. Pour in the egg mixture and cook for 3-4 minutes until the omelette is set underneath. Meanwhile preheat the grill to moderate.

4 Place the pan under the grill for 2-3 minutes until the omelette is set on top, but still moist in the middle.

5 Serve cut into wedges, with a crisp salad and crusty bread.

TURKEY TIKKA

SERVES 4

You can buy ready prepared tikka paste in jars; tikka powder is equally suitable. Leave the turkey to marinate for longer than suggested if you have time.

150 ml (¼ pint) natural yogurt
3 tablespoons tikka paste
2 cloves garlic, crushed
1 tablespoon sunflower oil
1 tablespoon lemon juice
625 g (1¼ lb) boneless turkey, skinned and cut into chunks
shredded lettuce to serve

ONION SALAD
½ cucumber, sliced
1 onion, thinly sliced
1 tablespoon chopped coriander leaves
2 tablespoons wine vinegar
1 tablespoon sunflower oil

1 Mix the yogurt with the tikka paste, garlic, oil and lemon juice until well blended.

2 Put the turkey chunks into a shallow dish, cover with the yogurt mixture and turn the turkey chunks until they are well coated. Leave to marinate for 20 minutes.

3 To make the salad, mix all the ingredients together in a bowl and leave for 20 minutes.

4 Preheat the grill to medium. Thread the turkey chunks on to 4 skewers and grill for 8-10 minutes, basting with the marinade and turning occasionally, until beginning to char.

5 Serve on a bed of shredded lettuce with the onion salad and naan bread.

CHICKEN & AVOCADO TOSTADOS

SERVES 4-8

In Mexico, tostados are hot and spicy but these are only moderately so. You can, of course, add more chilli powder if you prefer. Serve one or two tostados per person depending on appetite.

2 tablespoons oil
1 large onion, chopped
2 cloves garlic, chopped
1 teaspoon ground cumin
¼ teaspoon chilli powder
2 x 425 g (15 oz) cans borlotti beans
150 ml (¼ pint) tomato juice
1 tablespoon tomato purée
175 g (6 oz) cooked chicken, chopped
1 tablespoon chopped coriander leaves
salt and pepper to taste
8 tostado shells
1 avocado
4 tomatoes, sliced

TO GARNISH
coriander sprigs

1 Preheat oven to 190°C (375°F/Gas 5).

2 Heat the oil in a pan, add the onion and garlic and fry until softened, then add the spices and fry, stirring, for 1 minute.

3 Drain the borlotti beans. Add half of them to the spice mixture and mash with a potato masher. Add the tomato juice, tomato purée, chicken and coriander with the remaining beans. Add seasoning and stir well. Heat through, stirring occasionally, for 2-3 minutes.

4 Heat the tostado shells in the oven for 5 minutes to crispen. Halve, peel and slice the avocado.

5 Put a heaped spoonful of the fried bean mixture on each tostado shell. Top with slices of tomato and avocado and garnish with coriander to serve.

VARIATION Sprinkle the tostados with grated Cheddar cheese and serve with a leafy salad.

RAGOÛT OF CHICKEN WITH CARDAMOM

SERVES 4

If you can't get oyster mushrooms, use double the quantity of button mushrooms.

2 tablespoons olive oil
1 onion, chopped
350 g (12 oz) boneless chicken breast, cut into
   1 cm (½ inch) cubes
250 g (8 oz) button mushrooms
250 g (8 oz) oyster mushrooms
2 cloves garlic, chopped
2 tablespoons flour
125 ml (4 fl oz) milk
½ teaspoon cardamom seeds
salt and pepper to taste
125 ml (4 fl oz) double cream
400 g (14 oz) can haricot beans, drained
2 tablespoons chopped parsley
8 garlic croûtes (see below)

1   Heat the oil in a frying pan and fry the onion and chicken until sealed.

2   Add the mushrooms and garlic and fry, stirring occasionally, for a further 3 minutes.

3   Remove from the heat and stir in the flour, then stir in milk, cardamom and seasoning. Bring to the boil; cook, stirring, for 3 minutes until thickened.

4   Stir in the cream, beans and parsley. Heat through and serve with the garlic croûtes.

GARLIC CROÛTES: Slice a small French stick diagonally into 1 cm (½ inch) slices. Beat 50 g (2 oz) butter with 1 crushed garlic clove and 2 teaspoons chopped parsley. Toast bread on one side. Spread the untoasted side with garlic butter and toast again.

CHICKEN & SWEETCORN CHOWDER

SERVES 4

You can use creamed sweetcorn which gives a slightly sweet flavour if you prefer.

1 tablespoon sunflower oil
1 onion, chopped
1 clove garlic, chopped
2 medium potatoes, diced
600 ml (1 pint) chicken stock
1 bay leaf
salt and pepper to taste
300 g (11 oz) can sweetcorn, drained
175 g (6 oz) cooked chicken, chopped
2 tablespoons chopped parsley

1   Heat the oil in a pan, add the onion and garlic and fry until softened.

2   Add the potatoes, stock, bay leaf and seasoning and cook for 15 minutes.

3   Stir in the sweetcorn, chicken and parsley, and simmer gently for a further 5 minutes. Serve with crusty bread.

ABOVE: CHICKEN & SWEETCORN CHOWDER   *BELOW:* RAGOÛT OF CHICKEN WITH CARDAMOM

EVERYDAY MEALS

There are so many different inexpensive cuts of poultry available which offer an economical choice for everyday meals. Turkey mince is a low fat alternative to minced beef. It makes a very good chilli, and is excellent in a strong flavoured tomato sauce with pasta.

Chicken and turkey cubes are ideal for pies and curries; thighs and legs for casseroles; strips for stir frys. I have also included many suggestions for using leftover cooked poultry in this section. Drumsticks and wings are the perfect finger food – ideal for both picnics and barbecues.

CONTENTS

CHICKEN & POTATO CASSEROLE

SERVES 4

350 g (12 oz) baby new potatoes
salt and pepper to taste
2 tablespoons olive oil
4 chicken legs
125 g (4 oz) bacon steak, cut into strips
125 g (4 oz) pickling onions, or quartered small
   onions
2 cloves garlic, crushed
2 tablespoons flour
450 ml (¾ pint) chicken stock
75 g (3 oz) button mushrooms
50g (2 oz) stoned green olives
1 bay leaf
1 tablespoon chopped parsley

1   Preheat oven to 180°C (350°F/Gas 4). Parboil the potatoes in a pan of boiling salted water for 10 minutes; drain.

2   Heat the oil in a flameproof casserole, add the chicken and fry over a brisk heat, turning once, until golden brown. Remove from the pan.

3   Add the bacon and onions to the casserole and cook until golden.

4   Stir in the garlic and flour, then gradually add the stock and cook for 2 minutes, gently stirring until thickened.

5   Return the chicken to the casserole. Add the potatoes, mushrooms, olives, bay leaf and seasoning. Return to the boil.

6   Cover and cook in the oven for 30-40 minutes until the chicken is tender. Sprinkle with parsley and serve with a green vegetable.

CHICKEN WITH CAPERS & BACON

SERVES 4

A piquant sauce made with capers and bacon covers succulent chicken breasts. You can use chicken legs if you prefer, but you will need to increase the cooking time by 5 minutes.

2 tablespoons olive oil
4 skinless chicken breasts
1 onion, chopped
50 g (2 oz) smoked streaky bacon, chopped
1 tablespoon flour
175 g (6 oz) chicken stock
1 tablespoon tomato purée
1 tablespoon capers
1 tablespoon chopped parsley
salt and pepper to taste

TO GARNISH
parsley sprigs

1   Heat the oil in a pan, add the chicken breasts and fry, turning, for about 10 minutes until evenly coloured. Remove from the pan with a slotted spoon and keep warm.

2   Add the onion and bacon to the pan and fry for 4 minutes, then mix in the flour.

3   Gradually add the stock and tomato purée. Bring to the boil, stirring, and cook until thickened. Add the capers and chicken. Cover and simmer for a further 10 minutes until the chicken is cooked.

4   Add the parsley and seasoning. Serve garnished with parsley and accompanied by noodles or boiled potatoes.

ABOVE: CHICKEN & POTATO CASSEROLE   *BELOW*: CHICKEN WITH CAPERS & BACON

CHICKEN, LEEK & HAM FLAN

SERVES 4-6

Flans are always popular and this one is equally good served hot or cold, with a green salad. Use a deep flan ring.

25 g (1 oz) butter
1 tablespoon olive oil
500 g (1 lb) leeks, thinly sliced
4 tablespoons chicken stock
6 tablespoons single cream
3 eggs
175 g (6 oz) cooked chicken, chopped
50 g (2 oz) smoked ham, chopped
salt and pepper to taste
250 g (8 oz) ready-made shortcrust pastry
25 g (1 oz) fresh breadcrumbs

1 Preheat oven to 200°C (400°F/Gas 6).

2 Melt the butter with the oil in a heavy based pan and fry the leeks, stirring occasionally, for 5 minutes.

3 Add the stock, cover and cook gently for a further 5 minutes, then turn into a bowl.

4 Mix in the cream, eggs, chicken, ham and seasoning; set aside.

5 Roll out the pastry thinly and use to line a deep 23 cm (9 inch) fluted flan ring, standing on a thick baking sheet. Freeze for 5 minutes.

6 Pour the filling into the flan case, sprinkle with the breadcrumbs and bake for 35-40 minutes until set and golden brown.

TURKEY & CRANBERRY PIE

SERVES 4

A very useful recipe at Christmas time to use up leftover turkey and ham.

2 tablespoons sunflower oil
1 onion, chopped
1 clove garlic, chopped
125 g (4 oz) mushrooms, sliced
2 tablespoons flour
225 ml (8 fl oz) milk
50 g (2 oz) frozen cranberries
2 tablespoons chopped parsley
300 g (10 oz) cooked turkey, cut into chunks
125 g (4 oz) piece cooked ham, cut into cubes
salt and pepper to taste
6 sheets filo pastry
15 g (½ oz) melted butter

1 Preheat oven to 200°C (400°/Gas 6).

2 Heat the oil in a pan, add the onion and fry gently until softened. Add the garlic and mushrooms and cook for 3 minutes. Stir in the flour, then gradually add the milk and cook, gently stirring, until thickened.

3 Off the heat, stir in the frozen cranberries, parsley, turkey, ham and seasoning. Turn into a shallow 1.2 litre (2 pint) ovenproof dish.

4 Layer the filo sheets on top, brushing each one with melted butter. Trim off excess pastry with scissors. Before cooking, cut through the filo pastry, marking the pie into quarters, with a sharp knife.

5 Bake for 20-25 minutes until golden brown. Serve immediately.

CHICKEN WITH TOMATO & PARMESAN

SERVES 4

A quick and delicious Italian dish. Use one of the ready-prepared bottled tomato sauces to save time, but use with care – most of them have quite a strong flavour.

1 tablespoon olive oil
25 g (1 oz) butter
4 boneless chicken breasts, skinned
25 g (1 oz) flour
225 ml (8 fl oz) milk
50 g (2 oz) Parmesan cheese, freshly grated
salt and pepper to taste
2 tablespoons bottled Italian tomato sauce
1 tablespoon chopped basil

1 Heat the oil and butter in a heavy based pan. Add the chicken and fry gently, turning occasionally, for 10 minutes until cooked. Place in a serving dish and keep warm.

2 Add the flour to the buttery juices in the pan and mix together. Gradually stir in the milk. Bring to the boil and cook, stirring constantly, until thickened. Stir in half of the Parmesan and add seasoning.

3 Preheat the grill to high. Put a spoonful of tomato sauce on each chicken breast. Sprinkle with basil, then coat with the cheese sauce.

4 Sprinkle with the remaining Parmesan and grill until the topping is golden brown. Serve immediately, with a salad.

CHICKEN & BROCCOLI AU GRATIN

SERVES 4

Quick, tasty and simple to prepare. Make sure you only boil the broccoli briefly or it will become too soft when cooked in the oven.

500 g (1 lb) broccoli, divided into florets
2 x 300 g (10 oz) cans condensed chicken soup
75 g (3 oz) Parmesan cheese, freshly grated
350 g (12 oz) cooked chicken, chopped
2 tablespoons fresh breadcrumbs

1 Preheat oven to 190°C (375°F/Gas 5).

2 Cook the broccoli in boiling salted water for 3 minutes, then drain thoroughly.

3 Arrange the broccoli in a buttered gratin dish, cover with one can of condensed soup and sprinkle with half of the cheese.

4 Arrange the chicken in a layer on top and cover with the second can of soup.

5 Sprinkle with the remaining cheese and breadcrumbs. Cook in the oven for 20 minutes until golden brown. Serve immediately.

ABOVE: CHICKEN & BROCCOLI AU GRATIN *BELOW*: CHICKEN WITH TOMATO & PARMESAN

CHICKEN RISOTTO

SERVES 4

This Venetian risotto should have a creamy consistency. I sometimes make it with leftover chicken, in which case I mix the chicken into the rice with the olives.

---

3 tablespoons olive oil
350 g (12 oz) boneless chicken breast, skinned and cut into 2.5 cm (1 inch) cubes
1 onion, chopped
2 cloves garlic, chopped
300 g (10 oz) Italian risotto rice
600 ml (1 pint) chicken stock
150 ml (¼ pint) white wine
225 ml (8 fl oz) passata
2 teaspoons chopped oregano or ½ teaspoon dried
salt and pepper to taste
50 g (2 oz) black olives, halved and stoned
2 sun dried tomatoes, sliced
50 g (2 oz) Parmesan cheese, shredded

TO GARNISH
oregano sprigs

1. Heat the oil in a heavy based pan, add the chicken, onion and garlic and fry, stirring, for 5 minutes.

2. Add the rice, stock, wine, passata, oregano and seasoning, and bring to the boil.

3. Cover and cook gently for 25 minutes until the liquid is absorbed and the rice is just tender.

4. Remove from the heat and fork in the olives and sun dried tomatoes. Turn into a heated serving dish and sprinkle with the Parmesan. Garnish with oregano to serve.

SPAGHETTI WITH DOLCELATTE & CHICKEN

SERVES 4

350 g (12 oz) spaghetti
150 ml (¼ pint) soured cream
125 g (4 oz) dolcelatte, chopped
3 tablespoons chopped chives
125 g (4 oz) cooked chicken, chopped
salt and pepper to taste

TO GARNISH
chives

1. Bring a large pan of salted water to the boil. Add the spaghetti, stir once and boil for 10-12 minutes until tender.

2. Drain the spaghetti thoroughly, then return to the pan. Add the soured cream, dolcelatte, chives, chicken and seasoning. Heat through very gently, stirring constantly.

3. Serve immediately, garnished with chives and accompanied by a green salad.

ABOVE: SPAGHETTI WITH DOLCELATTE & CHICKEN *BELOW*: CHICKEN RISOTTO

TAGLIATELLE WITH CHICKEN & MUSHROOMS

SERVES 4

Porcini – Italian dried mushrooms – give this dish a really delicious flavour, but you can replace them with an extra 50 g (2 oz) chestnut mushrooms.

350-400 g (12-14 oz) fresh or dried tagliatelle
25 g (1 oz) porcini, soaked in boiling water for
* 20 minutes*
1 tablespoon olive oil
25 g (1 oz) butter
250 g (8 oz) boneless chicken breast, skinned and
* cut into strips*
175 g (6 oz) chestnut mushrooms, sliced
2 cloves garlic, chopped
1 tablespoon flour
150 ml (¼ pint) double cream
2 tablespoons chopped parsley
salt and pepper to taste

1 Bring a large pan of salted water to the boil. Add the pasta, stir once and boil for 3-4 minutes for fresh, 8-10 minutes for dried, until tender.

2 Meanwhile drain and slice the soaked mushrooms, reserving 6 tablespoons liquid.

3 Heat the oil and butter in a pan, add the chicken and fry, stirring, until sealed.

4 Add the dried and fresh mushrooms with the garlic and cook, stirring occasionally, for 5 minutes. Stir in the flour, then add the reserved mushroom liquid and cook, stirring, until thickened.

5 Stir in the cream, parsley and seasoning, and heat through.

6 Drain the pasta thoroughly and toss with the mushroom sauce. Serve with a salad.

PASTA WITH CHICKEN & OLIVES

SERVES 4

The wonderful rich flavours of sun dried tomatoes, black olives, garlic and basil are set off simply with a bowl of pasta. Sprinkle with freshly grated Parmesan to serve if you like.

250 g (8 oz) dried pasta shapes
1 tablespoon olive oil
250 g (8 oz) boneless chicken breast, skinned and
* cut into thin strips*
2 cloves garlic
125 g (4 oz) black olives, halved and stoned
4 sun dried tomatoes in oil, thinly sliced
salt and pepper to taste
2 tablespoons chopped basil

TO GARNISH
basil sprigs

1 Bring a large pan of salted water to the boil. Add the pasta and bring back to the boil. Reduce the heat and simmer for 8-10 minutes or according to packet instructions, stirring occasionally.

2 Meanwhile heat the oil in a frying pan, add the chicken and fry, stirring occasionally, until sealed and golden.

3 Add the garlic, olives and sun dried tomatoes, with a tablespoon of their oil, and heat through.

4 Drain the pasta well and mix with the tomato mixture. Season and turn on to warmed serving plates. Sprinkle with the chopped basil. Garnish with sprigs of basil and serve with a green salad.

ABOVE: TAGLIATELLE WITH CHICKEN & MUSHROOMS   *BELOW*: PASTA WITH CHICKEN & OLIVES

DUCK CASSOULET

SERVES 4

I often use canned beans and they are ideal for this extremely quick, tasty alternative to a traditionally prepared cassoulet. I like to serve it with a crisp green salad.

2 duck breasts
oil for brushing
175 g (6 oz) smoked bacon steaks
3 x 400 g (14 oz) cans haricot beans, drained
250 g (8 oz) garlic sausage, sliced
300 ml (½ pint) bottled Italian tomato sauce
125 ml (4 fl oz) chicken stock
2 cloves garlic
salt and pepper to taste
40 g (1½ oz) fresh breadcrumbs

1 Preheat oven to 190°C (375°F/Gas 5) and preheat the grill to medium.

2 Place the duck breasts skin side down on a rack in the grill pan, brush with oil and grill for 3 minutes. Turn the duck over and cook for a further 5 minutes until the skin crispens and most of the fat has run out. Add the bacon steaks to the grill rack for the last 3 minutes, turning once.

3 Slice the duck and bacon steaks thickly and put into a bowl with the beans, garlic sausage, tomato sauce, stock, garlic and seasoning.

4 Mix together thoroughly and turn into a deep earthenware casserole. Sprinkle with the breadcrumbs and bake for 30 minutes.

PAPRIKA TURKEY

SERVES 4

I usually serve this with noodles, but plain boiled potatoes are also very good with the paprika sauce.

2 tablespoons sunflower oil
625 g (1¼ lb) turkey cubes
1 onion, sliced
2 cloves garlic, chopped
1 red pepper, cored, seeded and sliced
1 tablespoon paprika
1 tablespoon flour
225 ml (8 fl oz) chicken stock
1 teaspoon caraway seeds
400 g (14 oz) can chopped tomatoes
salt and pepper to taste
150 ml (¼ pint) soured cream
1 tablespoon chopped parsley

1 Heat the oil in a pan, add the turkey cubes and fry, stirring, until sealed on all sides, then remove from the pan.

2 Add the onion, garlic and pepper to the pan and cook for 5 minutes.

3 Stir in the paprika and flour and cook for 30 seconds, then stir in the stock. Add the caraway seeds, tomatoes and seasoning. Return the turkey to the pan. Cover and cook for 20 minutes until tender.

4 Turn into a serving dish. Gently warm the soured cream, then pour over the turkey mixture. Sprinkle with parsley and serve with noodles or potatoes.

ABOVE: DUCK CASSOULET *BELOW*: PAPRIKA TURKEY

CHICKEN FRICASSÉE

SERVES 4

A very useful recipe for using up leftover chicken or turkey. You can also add sliced green or red peppers, peas or sweetcorn, for a change.

40 g (1½ oz) butter
1 onion, chopped
175 g (6 oz) mushrooms, sliced
½ teaspoon paprika
25 g (1 oz) flour
300 ml (½ pint) chicken stock
350 g (12 oz) cooked chicken, cut into chunks
120 ml (4 fl oz) single cream
salt and pepper to taste
1 tablespoon chopped chervil or parsley
chervil or parsley sprigs to garnish

1 Heat the butter in a pan and fry the onion until softened. Add the mushrooms and cook for a further 2 minutes.

2 Stir in the paprika and flour and cook for 30 seconds, then gradually stir in the stock. Bring to the boil and cook, stirring, for 2 minutes, until thickened.

3 Add the chicken, cream and seasoning, and heat gently for a few minutes.

4 Turn into a serving dish and sprinkle with chopped chervil or parsley. Garnish with sprigs of chervil or parsley and serve with boiled rice.

MEDITERRANEAN CHICKEN

SERVES 4

A rich sauce of peppers, tomatoes and olives cooked with goujons of chicken. Sun dried tomatoes enhance the Mediterranean flavour.

3 tablespoons olive oil
1 small onion, thinly sliced
350 g (12 oz) chicken goujons
2 cloves garlic, chopped
1 small red pepper, cored, seeded and thinly sliced
1 small green pepper, cored, seeded and thinly sliced
400 g (14 oz) can chopped tomatoes
4 sun dried tomatoes in oil, drained and thinly sliced
50 g (2 oz) black olives, halved and stoned
salt and pepper to taste
2 tablespoons chopped basil
basil sprigs to garnish

1 Heat the oil in a heavy based pan and fry the onion and chicken together, stirring occasionally, until the chicken is sealed.

2 Add the garlic and peppers, and cook for a further 4 minutes, stirring occasionally.

3 Add the chopped tomatoes, sun dried tomatoes, olives and seasoning. Cover and cook for 5 minutes.

4 Stir in the basil. Serve garnished with sprigs of basil and accompanied by rice or crusty bread.

CHICKEN MASALA

SERVES 4

A delicious, mild curry – best served with plain boiled basmati rice and mango chutney. I often make it with leftover cooked chicken – simply cut into chunks and add to the coconut sauce, reducing the cooking time to 5 minutes.

2 tablespoons sunflower oil
500 g (1 lb) boneless chicken breast, skinned and
  cut into cubes
1 onion, chopped
2 cloves garlic, crushed
1/2 teaspoon ground cumin
1 teaspoon ground coriander
1 teaspoon turmeric
seeds from 4 cardamom pods
2 teaspoons finely chopped fresh root ginger
25 g (1 oz) creamed coconut, blended with
  185 ml (6 fl oz) boiling water
salt to taste
150 ml (1/4 pint) double cream
1 tablespoon chopped coriander leaves

TO GARNISH
coriander sprigs

1 Heat the oil in a heavy based pan, add the chicken and fry, stirring, until sealed all over. Remove from the pan.

2 Add the onion to the pan and fry until softened, then add the garlic, spices and ginger; fry for 1 minute, stirring constantly.

3 Return the chicken to the pan. Add the coconut liquid with salt. Cover and simmer for 15 minutes.

4 Stir in the cream and chopped coriander and cook for 3 minutes. Serve with rice, garnished with coriander sprigs.

TURKEY CHILLI

SERVES 4

Turkey mince is quick to cook and available from most supermarkets. Add more chilli powder if you like a really hot chilli.

2 tablespoons olive oil
1 onion, chopped
500 g (1 lb) minced turkey
2 cloves garlic, chopped
1/4 teaspoon chilli powder
1 teaspoon ground cumin
1 tablespoon flour
120 ml (4 fl oz) chicken stock
175 g (6 oz) can red peppers, drained and sliced
400 g (14 oz) can chopped tomatoes
1 tablespoon tomato purée
salt and pepper to taste
2 x 400 g (14 oz) cans red kidney beans, drained
1 tablespoon chopped parsley

1 Heat the oil in a pan, add the onion and fry until softened. Add the turkey and garlic and fry briskly, stirring, until sealed all over.

2 Add the spices and flour and cook, stirring, for 1 minute. Stir in the stock, red peppers, tomatoes, tomato purée and seasoning, and bring to the boil.

3 Cover and cook for 20 minutes, then stir in the beans and parsley and heat through.

CHICKEN CHOW MEIN

SERVES 4

175 g (6 oz) Chinese egg noodles
2 teaspoons sesame oil
2 eggs
salt and pepper to taste
2 tablespoons groundnut oil
350 g (12 oz) chicken breast strips
1 clove garlic, chopped
2.5 cm (1 inch) fresh root ginger, chopped
1 red pepper, cored, seeded and thinly sliced
125 g (4 oz) shiitake or chestnut mushrooms,
  sliced
6-8 spring onions, cut into 3.5 cm (1½ inch)
  lengths
2 tablespoons sherry
2 tablespoons soy sauce
50 g (2 oz) roasted cashew nuts

1 Cook the noodles in boiling salted water according to packet instructions. Drain well and toss in the sesame oil.

2 Beat the eggs with seasoning in a bowl. Heat 1 teaspoon oil in a frying pan, pour in half the egg mixture to make a large thin omelette and cook on both sides. Turn out and cut into strips. Repeat with the remaining egg.

3 Heat the remaining oil in a wok and stir fry the chicken for 2 minutes; remove.

4 Add the garlic, ginger, red pepper, mushrooms and spring onions and stir fry for 2 minutes.

5 Add the noodles, sherry, soy sauce and chicken and cook, stirring, for 2 minutes.

6 Stir in the egg strips and cashew nuts and heat through. Serve immediately.

CHICKEN WITH BLACK BEAN SAUCE

SERVES 4

A colourful stir fry with a piquant black bean sauce. Serve with noodles or rice.

4 tablespoons sherry
6 tablespoons black bean sauce
4 tablespoons chicken stock or water
1 teaspoon cornflour
3 tablespoons groundnut oil 350 g (12 oz)
  boneless chicken breast, cut into thin strips
1 bunch spring onions, cut into 2.5 cm (1 inch)
  lengths
125 g (4 oz) baby corn cobs, halved lengthwise
125 g (4 oz) mangetout, topped and tailed
1 red pepper, cored, seeded and thinly sliced
2 cloves garlic, chopped

1 In a bowl, mix together the sherry, black bean sauce, stock or water and cornflour until smooth.

2 Heat half the oil in a wok and stir fry the chicken briskly until sealed all over. Remove from the wok and keep warm.

3 Add the remaining oil to the wok. Add the spring onions, baby corn, mangetout, red pepper and garlic and stir fry for 2 minutes.

4 Return the chicken to the wok and add the cornflour mixture. Cook, stirring, until thickened. Turn on to a warmed serving dish and serve with Chinese noodles or rice.

TERIYAKI TURKEY

SERVES 4

For this dish you need bamboo satay sticks. Soak them in water before use, to prevent them catching under the grill.

500 g (1 lb) turkey strips

MARINADE
3 tablespoons soy sauce
2 tablespoons sherry
2 cloves garlic, crushed
2.5 cm (1 inch) piece fresh root ginger, finely chopped
1 tablespoon sesame oil

FRIED RICE
2 tablespoons sunflower oil
6 spring onions, chopped
2 teaspoons ground cumin
500 g (1 lb) cooked rice

1 Mix the marinade ingredients together in a shallow dish. Add the turkey strips, turn to coat and leave to marinate for 30 minutes.

2 To make the fried rice, heat the oil in a frying pan and stir fry the spring onions for 2 minutes. Add the cumin and fry, stirring, for 1 minute. Add the rice and turn to coat with the spiced oil. Heat through gently, stirring. Cover and keep warm.

3 Preheat the grill to high. Thread the turkey on to bamboo satay sticks to resemble snakes, using about 3 strips to each stick. Grill for about 2 minutes on each side. Serve with the fried rice, and accompanied by a salad.

SWEET & SOUR CHICKEN

SERVES 4

2 tablespoons wine vinegar
1 tablespoon clear honey
1 tablespoon soy sauce
2 tablespoons tomato ketchup
1 tablespoon cornflour
salt and pepper to taste
200 g (7 oz) can pineapple chunks in syrup
2 tablespoons groundnut oil
350 g (12 oz) boneless chicken breast, cut into chunks
2 cloves garlic, chopped
1 red pepper, cored, seeded and cut into 2.5 cm (1 inch) squares
1 green pepper, cored, seeded and cut into 2.5 cm (1 inch) squares
1 onion, chopped

1 In a bowl mix together the vinegar, honey, soy sauce, tomato ketchup, cornflour and seasoning until smooth. Drain the pineapple and set aside, reserving the syrup; make up to 175 ml (6 fl oz) with water, then add to the bowl.

2 Heat the oil in a pan and stir fry the chicken for 3-4 minutes until golden. Remove from the pan.

3 Add the garlic, peppers and onion to the pan and stir fry for 4 minutes.

4 Add the cornflour mixture with the chicken and pineapple and cook, stirring, until thickened. Simmer for 3 minutes. Serve with boiled rice.

ENTERTAINING

I often use duck breasts, chicken breasts and turkey steaks for entertaining – they look attractive and are versatile, giving you plenty of scope to be creative. Try turkey fillet with cranberries, poulet à la Normande, or duck breasts with kumquats.

Poussins are also ideal for entertaining. Half a poussin looks attractive on a plate – much more appealing than a chicken quarter. Poussins can be barbecued, fried or grilled equally well. Try poussins with lemon & grapes or barbecued poussins for elegant dinner parties.

CONTENTS

POULET À LA NORMANDE

SERVES 4

A rich dish using cream, cider and apples;
ingredients that abound in Normandy.

2 tablespoons olive oil
2 dessert apples, peeled, cored and sliced into
rings
4 skinned chicken breasts
1 tablespoon flour
225 ml (8 fl oz) medium cider
salt and pepper to taste
125 ml (4 fl oz) double cream
1 tablespoon chopped chervil or parsley

TO GARNISH
chervil or parsley sprigs

1 Heat the oil in a frying pan, add the apple slices
and fry on both sides until turning golden.
Remove from the pan and keep warm.

2 Add the chicken breasts to the pan and fry until
tinged with brown, turning once.

3 Stir in the flour, then add the cider and
seasoning and mix until blended. Bring to the
boil, cover and simmer for 10-15 minutes until the
chicken is cooked through.

4 Add the cream, chervil or parsley and apples to
the pan and heat through. Serve garnished with
chervil or parsley and accompanied by new potatoes
and a green vegetable.

TURKEY FILLET WITH CRANBERRIES

SERVES 4

The cooking time will vary, depending on the
thickness of the turkey steaks. Fresh or frozen
cranberries can be used.

2 tablespoons sunflower oil
1 onion, chopped
2 cloves garlic, chopped
4 turkey breast steaks
1 tablespoon flour
150 ml (¼ pint) chicken stock
salt and pepper to taste
6 tablespoons port
50 g (2 oz) cranberries
1 teaspoon redcurrant jelly
1 teaspoon red wine vinegar

TO GARNISH
parsley sprigs

1 Heat the oil in a pan, add the onion and fry until
softened. Add the garlic and turkey steaks and fry
on both sides until they are a pale golden colour.

2 Stir in the flour, then add the stock and
seasoning and bring to the boil, stirring.

3 Add the port, cranberries, redcurrant jelly and
vinegar. Cover and simmer for 10-15 minutes.

4 Garnish with parsley and serve with courgettes
or mangetout.

CHICKEN STROGANOFF

SERVES 4

A variation on the well known Russian dish, which uses steak.

350 g (12 oz) boneless chicken breast, skinned
25 g (1 oz) butter
1 tablespoon sunflower oil (approximately)
1 onion, thinly sliced
125 g (4 oz) mushrooms, sliced
2 cloves garlic, chopped
2 tablespoons chopped parsley
2 tablespoons brandy
salt and pepper to taste
150 ml (¼ pint) double cream

TO GARNISH
parsley sprigs

1 Cut the chicken breast into thin strips, about 5 mm (¼ inch) wide.

2 Heat half the butter with the oil in a frying pan, add the onion and fry slowly until softened.

3 Add the mushrooms and garlic to the pan and fry briskly for 2-3 minutes, adding more oil if necessary, then remove from the pan.

4 Melt the remaining butter in the pan, add the chicken strips and fry briskly for 3-4 minutes, stirring occasionally.

5 Return the onion mixture to the pan with the parsley, brandy and seasoning, and heat through. Stir in the cream and heat gently. Garnish with parsley and serve with rice flavoured with herbs.

CHICKEN WITH PRUNES

SERVES 4

You can soak the prunes for as little as 30 minutes, but if you are able to leave them longer, they will plump up nicely.

125 g (4 oz) pitted prunes
300 ml (½ pint) dry white wine
25 g (1 oz) butter
4 skinless chicken breasts
2 teaspoons cornflour
1 teaspoon lemon juice
2 teaspoons redcurrant jelly
120 ml (4 fl oz) double cream

TO GARNISH
chervil or parsley sprigs

1 Put the prunes in a bowl with the wine and leave to soak for 30 minutes, or longer if possible.

2 Heat the butter in a frying pan and fry the chicken on both sides until pale golden.

3 Add the prunes and wine to the pan, cover and simmer for 15-20 minutes.

4 Blend the cornflour with the lemon juice and a little water, then add to the pan with the redcurrant jelly and cook, gently stirring, for 1 minute until thickened.

5 Add the cream and heat through, then turn into a warmed serving dish. Garnish with chervil or parsley and serve with a green vegetable.

PAELLA

SERVES 4

For speed leave the shells on the mussels, but if you have the time, remove the empty half shell when cooked. This enables the mussels to be eaten far more easily.

---

3 tablespoons olive oil
350 g (12 oz) boneless chicken breast, cut into
   chunks
1 onion, chopped
175 g (6 oz) cleaned squid, cut into rings
3 cloves garlic, chopped
300 g (10 oz) Valencian rice or Italian risotto
   rice
175 g (6 oz) can red peppers, drained and sliced
2 beefsteak tomatoes, skinned and chopped
600 ml (1 pint) chicken stock
few saffron strands, soaked in 2 tablespoons
   boiling water
salt and pepper to taste
16 mussels
125 g (4 oz) shelled prawns
2 tablespoons chopped parsley

TO GARNISH
8 cooked prawns in shell
lemon wedges
parsley sprigs

1 Preheat oven to 180°C (350°F/Gas 4).

2 Heat the oil in a paella pan or flameproof casserole. Add the chicken and fry until sealed all over; remove from the pan.

3 Add the onion, squid and garlic to the pan and fry for 5 minutes, stirring occasionally.

4 Return the chicken to the pan. Stir in the rice, peppers and tomatoes with the stock. Add the saffron with its liquid, and seasoning. Bring to the boil and simmer for 10 minutes.

5 Meanwhile scrub the mussels in cold water and remove their beards; discard any with open or damaged shells.

6 Bury the mussels in the rice and cook in the oven for 15 minutes or until the stock is absorbed.

7 Mix the prawns into the paella and remove the empty half shell from each mussel if desired. Discard any unopened mussels.

8 Sprinkle with parsley and garnish the paella with whole prawns, lemon wedges and parsley sprigs to serve.

CHICKEN WITH MUSTARD & CIDER SAUCE

SERVES 4

Cider, mustard and cream combine to give a delicious, piquant sauce for an extremely quick dish. Turkey breast steaks can also be used for this recipe.

1 tablespoon olive oil
4 skinless chicken breasts
2 cloves garlic, chopped
2 teaspoons cornflour
125 ml (4 fl oz) medium cider
2 tablespoons coarse grain (Meaux) mustard
4 tablespoons double cream
4 spring onions, diagonally sliced
salt and pepper to taste

1 Heat the oil in a heavy based pan and add the chicken breasts with the garlic. Fry the chicken on both sides until beginning to turn brown.

2 Blend the cornflour with a little of the cider; adding the rest of the cider to the pan. Cover and simmer gently for 5 minutes.

3 Stir in the blended cornflour, mustard, cream, spring onions and seasoning. Cook, gently stirring, until thickened.

4 Spoon into a warmed serving dish and serve with new potatoes or rice, and a green vegetable.

DUCK BREASTS WITH KUMQUATS

SERVES 4

I like to serve this recipe with braised chicory and new potatoes.

50 g (2 oz) kumquats
1 tablespoon oil
1 onion, chopped
2 tablespoons flour
225 ml (8 fl oz) duck or chicken stock
125 ml (4 fl oz) red wine
1 teaspoon soy sauce
1 tablespoon redcurrant jelly
4 duck breasts, about 150 g (5oz) each
salt and pepper to taste

TO GARNISH
watercress sprigs

1 Thinly slice half the kumquats, removing as many pips as possible; chop the rest finely.

2 Heat the oil in a pan, add the onion and fry until softened. Add the chopped kumquats with the flour; stir well.

3 Stir in the stock and wine. Cover and simmer for 10 minutes, then sieve and return to the pan. Add the soy sauce, redcurrant jelly, sliced kumquats and seasoning. Simmer gently for 5 minutes.

4 Preheat grill to medium. Place the duck breasts skin side down on a rack in the grill pan, brush with oil and grill for 3-4 minutes. Turn the duck and cook for a further 5-7 minutes until the skin crispens, but the flesh is still slightly pink.

5 Slice the duck breasts thinly and arrange each one in a fan shape on a warmed serving plate. Spoon over the kumquat sauce and garnish with watercress to serve.

ABOVE: DUCK BREASTS WITH KUMQUATS *BELOW*: CHICKEN WITH MUSTARD & CIDER SAUCE

DUCK WITH MANGO & GINGER

SERVES 4

2 tablespoons soy sauce
2 tablespoons sherry
4 duck breasts, skinned and thinly sliced
2 teaspoons cornflour
1 mango
2 tablespoons groundnut oil
1 bunch spring onions, cut into 4 cm (1½ inch) lengths
2 cloves garlic, chopped
2.5 cm (1 inch) piece fresh root ginger, finely chopped
15 cm (6 inch) piece cucumber, halved and thickly sliced

1. Mix the soy sauce and sherry in a small bowl. Add the duck and stir well to coat, then leave to marinate for 10 minutes. Remove the duck from the marinade and set aside.

2. Blend the cornflour with the marinade and 3 tablespoons water.

3. Cut the mango on either side of the stone, then peel and cut into slices.

4. Heat the oil in a wok or frying pan and stir fry the duck for 3 minutes, then remove.

5. Add the spring onions, garlic, ginger and cucumber to the pan and stir fry for 2 minutes.

6. Return the duck to the pan, stir in the cornflour mixture and cook until thickened.

7. Add the mango slices and heat through. Serve with noodles or boiled rice.

CRISPY DUCK PANCAKES

SERVES 4

A quick version of the popular Peking duck. Allow time to roast the duck but everything else can be prepared in minutes. Buy the Chinese pancakes in Oriental food stores; they are usually sold frozen in packets and only need defrosting and steaming.

1.5 kg (3½ lb) duck
½ cucumber
1 bunch spring onions
24 Chinese pancakes

SAUCE
4 tablespoons hoisin sauce
1 tablespoon soy sauce
1 tablespoon clear honey
2 teaspoons sesame oil

1. Preheat oven to 230°C (450°F/Gas 8). Put the duck on a rack in a roasting tin and cook for 15 minutes. Reduce the heat to 190°C (375°F/Gas 5) and cook for a further 1-1¼ hours.

2. Mix the sauce ingredients together and put into 4 small individual dishes.

3. Cut the cucumber and spring onions into fine strips and put into serving dishes.

4. Leave the duck to stand for 10 minutes before carving. Cut the skin and meat into pieces and arrange on a warmed platter.

5. Steam the pancakes over a pan of boiling water for 8-10 minutes.

6. To assemble each pancake, spread with a little sauce, add some duck skin and meat, then top with spring onions and cucumber. Roll up and eat!

ABOVE: DUCK WITH MANGO & GINGER *BELOW*: CRISPY DUCK PANCAKES

BARBECUED POUSSINS

SERVES 4

These can be barbecued or grilled equally well. Slash the poussins deeply before brushing on the sauce, so that they cook through more easily. For this quantity of cooked rice you will need 250 g (8 oz) raw weight.

2 poussins

BARBECUE SAUCE
2 tablespoons tomato ketchup
2 tablespoons fruit sauce
2 tablespoons coarse grain (Meaux) mustard
2 teaspooons Worcestershire sauce
1 teaspoon soy sauce

SPICED RICE
2 tablespoons sunflower oil
2 cloves garlic, chopped
½ teaspoon ground turmeric
1 teaspoon ground coriander
750 g (1½ lb) cooked rice

1 Using a sharp knife, cut each poussin through the breast and down either side of the backbone. Discard the backbone and slash the poussins in 2 or 3 places.

2 To prepare the barbecue sauce, mix the tomato ketchup, fruit sauce, mustard, Worcestershire and soy sauces together in a bowl until smooth.

3 Preheat the grill to medium. Brush the barbecue sauce over both sides of the poussins and grill for 10 minutes on each side, brushing with more sauce occasionally.

4 Meanwhile prepare the spiced rice. Heat the oil in a pan, add the garlic and spices and fry, stirring, for 1 minute. Stir in the rice and heat through, stirring occasionally.

5 Serve the grilled poussins with the spiced rice and accompanied by a crisp salad.

VARIATION For a more spicy flavour rub the poussins with a dry devil mixture and leave for 15 minutes before applying the barbecue sauce and grilling. To prepare the devil mixture, simply mix 1 teaspoon each of salt, ground ginger, dry mustard and curry powder with ¼ teaspoon chilli powder until evenly blended.

RIGHT: BARBECUED POUSSINS

POUSSINS WITH LEMON & GRAPES

SERVES 4

A poussin is a small succulent chicken. I find half a bird per person is ample, but you may prefer to serve a whole one.

2 poussins, about 500 g (1 lb) each
1 tablespoon sunflower oil
juice of 1 lemon
3 tablespoons chicken stock
salt and pepper to taste
150 ml (¼ pint) double cream
3 tablespoons chopped mixed herbs, e.g. chives, thyme, marjoram, parsley
125 g (4 oz) seedless green grapes, halved

TO GARNISH
chervil sprigs

1 Halve the poussins, by cutting through the breast then down each side of the backbone. Discard the backbone.

2 Heat the oil in a heavy based pan and fry the poussins for 5 minutes on each side until golden brown.

3 Add the lemon juice and stock to the pan, with seasoning. Cover and cook gently for 15 minutes.

4 Remove the poussins and keep warm. Add the cream, herbs and grapes to the pan and mix well to incorporate all the pan juices, then boil for 1 minute.

5 Arrange the poussins on warmed serving plates and spoon some sauce over each one. Garnish with chervil sprigs. Serve with a green vegetable.

CHICKEN WITH GREEN PEPPERCORNS

SERVES 4

A piquant sauce of wine vinegar, mustard and green peppercorns, mellowed by the addition of cream. Quite delicious!

1 tablespoon olive oil
2 cloves garlic, roughly chopped
4 chicken breasts
3 tablespoons wine vinegar
1 tablespoon Dijon mustard
1 tablespoon tomato purée
150 ml (¼ pint) double cream
1 teaspoon green peppercorns in brine, drained
salt and pepper to taste

TO GARNISH
chives

1 Heat the oil in a frying pan, add the garlic and chicken breasts and fry gently, turning occasionally, until the chicken is beginning to colour.

2 Add the wine vinegar, cover and cook gently for 15-20 minutes depending on the thickness of the chicken breasts.

3 Stir in the mustard, tomato purée, cream, peppercorns and seasoning, and stir well to combine evenly.

4 Cover and cook for a few minutes to heat through. Garnish with chives. Serve with new potatoes and broccoli.

CHICKEN WITH BACON IN TARRAGON SAUCE

SERVES 4

In this delicious concoction chicken breasts are wrapped in bacon and baked in cider. The juices are made into a creamy sauce, flavoured with tarragon.

8 rashers streaky bacon, rinds removed
4 boneless chicken breasts
175 ml (6 fl oz) cider
25 g (1 oz) butter
2 tablespoons flour
125 ml (4 fl oz) single cream
1 teaspoon chopped tarragon
salt and pepper to taste

1. Preheat oven to 200°C (400°F/Gas 6).

2. Wrap 2 bacon rashers around each chicken breast. Place them in a greased shallow ovenproof dish. Pour over the cider and bake in the oven for 20 minutes until cooked.

3. Pour off the juices and reserve; keep the chicken breasts warm.

4. Heat the butter in a small saucepan. Stir in the flour and cook, stirring, for 1 minute. Remove from the heat and mix in the reserved juices. Bring to the boil and cook, stirring continuously, for 2 minutes until thickened.

5. Stir in the cream and tarragon, with seasoning.

6. Pour the sauce over the chicken breasts and serve with new potatoes and a green vegetable.

CHICKEN WITH WILD MUSHROOMS

SERVES 4

This is one of my favourite meals, served with wild rice and a green salad. You can only achieve the necessary depth of flavour with cep mushrooms and, as they are rarely available fresh, I frequently use dried ones. Wild rice is expensive, but you can now buy a mixture of wild rice and brown rice which has a very good flavour.

25 g (1 oz) dried ceps, soaked in boiling water for
* 20 minutes*
2 tablespoons olive oil
1 onion, sliced
250 g (12 oz) chicken goujons
250 g (8 oz) chestnut mushrooms, sliced
1 tablespoon flour
6 tablespoons double cream

1. Drain the ceps, reserving 225 ml (8 fl oz) liquid; slice them, discarding the stalks.

2. Heat the oil in a frying pan, add the onion and chicken and fry, stirring, until the goujons are golden brown.

3. Add the ceps and chestnut mushrooms and fry for 3 minutes, stirring occasionally.

4. Stir in the flour, then add the reserved soaking liquid and bring to the boil, stirring. Cook for a further 5 minutes.

5. Add the cream and heat through. Serve with rice and a salad.

ABOVE: CHICKEN WITH BACON IN TARRAGON SAUCE; FEUILLETÉS WITH BROCCOLI & BOURSIN (PAGE 94)
BELOW: CHICKEN WITH WILD MUSHROOMS

FEUILLETÉS WITH BROCCOLI & BOURSIN

SERVES 4

Frozen puff pastry is just the right shape for making square vol au vents. Just a few rolls and each pack is large enough to make two. The Boursin melts to a rich garlicy sauce which coats the chicken and broccoli. Avoid overcooking the broccoli or it will break up when you fold it into the filling. Illustrated on previous page.

2 x 250 g (8 oz) packets puff pastry
beaten egg to glaze

FILLING
250 g (8 oz) broccoli florets
150 g (5 oz) Boursin cheese
90 ml (3 fl oz) single cream
salt and pepper to taste
250 g (8 oz) cooked chicken, cut into chunks
1 tablespoon chopped chives

1 | Preheat oven to 220°C (425°F/Gas 7).

2 | Roll out each piece of pastry on a lightly floured surface, to measure 13 x 25 cm (5 x 10 inches). Cut each rectangle in half to make 4 pastry squares. Trim the edges to neaten if necessary.

3 | Using a sharp knife, mark a 1 cm (½ inch) border within each rectangle, without cutting right through to the bottom; this will form the lid.

4 | Score the tops, brush with beaten egg and bake for 15-20 minutes, until well risen and golden.

5 | To make the filling, blanch the broccoli in boiling salted water for 3 minutes, then drain.

6 | Put the Boursin in a saucepan with the cream and seasoning. Heat gently, stirring frequently, until melted. Add the broccoli, chicken and chives and heat through gently.

7 | Carefully lift off the square of pastry from the centre of each vol au vent and scoop out the uncooked dough from the inside.

8 | Fill the vol au vent cases with the broccoli mixture and replace the lids. Serve immediately with a green salad.

VARIATION Replace the broccoli with cauliflower florets if you prefer.

INDEX